Arizona Activity Book

by Paula Ellis, illustrations by Shane Nitzsche

Dedicated to Gay Lynne Liebertz, who shared with me her love for the Southwest, the native peoples and the magnificent scenery she knew as a child.

~Paula

Cover design by Jonathan Norberg
Book design by Lora Westberg

10 9 8 7 6 5 4 3

Copyright 2012 by Paula Ellis
Published by Adventure Publications
An imprint of AdventureKEEN
(800) 678-7006
www.adventurepublications.net
All rights reserved
Printed in China

ISBN: 978-1-59193-288-8

Welcome to Arizona

Millions of years ago, the land we call Arizona was at the bottom of the ocean. Over time, the water moved back, the ground began to dry, and mountains rose high above the earth. The land became a mixture of mountains, trees, prairies, lakes and streams.

Ancient peoples came to the land thousands of years before any Spanish or European settlers did. These first people were hunters and farmers. No one knows for sure what happened, but they all disappeared. They may have run out of water and been forced to leave, or perhaps they did not survive.

Eventually, the land became populated with Native American tribes. Then, almost 500 years ago, Spanish explorers came up from Mexico. Priests set up churches, and some of the churches are still standing today. European settlers soon moved into the Arizona region from the East.

In 1846, Mexico fought against the U.S. in the Mexican-American War. After the war ended in 1848, much of the Arizona land became part of the United States. The rest was bought in 1853 by the U.S. ambassador to Mexico, James Gadsden, in the Gadsden Purchase.

Towns began to grow as people moved west to explore the new territory. Gold and silver mining, cattle ranches and the railroad brought more and more people to the region.

On February 24, 1863, President Abraham Lincoln signed a bill making this place the Territory of Arizona. And in 1912, Arizona became the 48th state to join the U.S. The name Arizona is believed to come from a Spanish word, *Arizonac*, meaning, "having a little spring."

Today, millions of tourists come every year to see the beauty, deserts, mountains, canyons and wonders of Arizona, which is nicknamed "the Grand Canyon State."

What do you want to do in Arizona?

☐ visit Hoover Dam   ☐ see the Grand Canyon   ☐ camp in Arizona parks
☐ eat a burrito   ☐ find a fossil   ☐ cross London Bridge
☐ fly over Meteor Crater   ☐ ride on Route 66   ☐ hike in Ramsey Canyon

Arizona Map

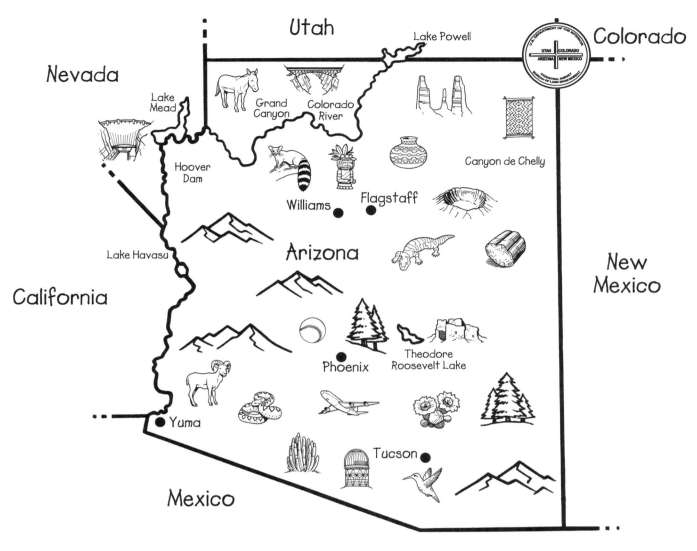

Use the map to find the answers.

What major river runs through Arizona?

☐ Rio Grande　　☐ Mississippi River　　☐ Colorado River　　☐ Snake River

How many states border Arizona? (hint: Mexico is not a state)

☐ 2　　　☐ 3　　　☐ 4　　　☐ 5　　　☐ 6

Circle the names of the states that border Arizona:

Hawaii	New Mexico	Mississippi	Minnesota	Nevada	New York
California	Delaware	Ohio	Alaska	Oregon	Florida
Oklahoma	Tennessee	Colorado	Kansas	West Virginia	Utah

(answers on page 62)

Arizona State Symbols

State Flag

State Mammal Ringtail

State Butterfly Two-tailed Swallowtail

State Bird Cactus Wren

State Reptile Arizona Ridge-nosed Rattlesnake

State Fish Apache Trout

State Flower Saguaro Cactus Blossom

State Gemstone Turquoise

State Amphibian Arizona Tree Frog

Arizona Fun Facts

On February 14, 1912, Arizona became the 48th U.S. state.

It would take 4,800,000 pennies to equal the amount of copper in the roof of Arizona's Capitol Building.

Prescott is the home of the "World's Oldest Rodeo," held yearly since 1888.

In the mid-1800s, the U.S. Army used camels to travel across the Arizona deserts.

The highest point in Arizona is Humphreys Peak. It is in the Coconino National Forest, north of Flagstaff. The peak is 12,633 feet above sea level, but you don't have to be a climber to reach the summit. You can get there by hiking up the Humphreys Trail.

The northeast corner of Arizona is the site of the Four Corners Monument. It is the only place in the country where you can be in four states at one time: Arizona, Colorado, New Mexico and Utah.

During the winter of 1972–1973, Sunrise Mountain received 400.9 inches of snow—over 30 feet! That's the state record for total snowfall in one season.

A one-armed explorer, John Wesley Powell, led the first scientific expedition through the Grand Canyon in 1869.

Ramsey Canyon is said to be the "Hummingbird Capital of the U.S." because at least 15 different kinds of hummingbirds can be found there.

Throughout history, the area of Arizona has been under the rule of Spain, Mexico, the Confederate States of America and the United States of America.

Many people who live in colder areas of the U.S. move to Arizona during winter. They are called "snowbirds."

In Arizona, it is against the law to let a donkey sleep in a bathtub.

June 29, 1994, was Arizona's hottest day on record. In Lake Havasu City, the temperature reached 128 degrees.

At the Cerreta Candy Company, in Glendale, kids can make their very own chocolate pizza.

People from Arizona are called Arizonans.

ABCs of Arizona

Take a trip through the alphabet in the State of Arizona.

A is for **Adventure** in 22 national parks and at 41 national landmarks

B is for **Biosphere 2**, an enclosed place where scientists study the earth

C is for **Cowboys**, who drive cattle and work on Arizona ranches

D is for all four U.S. **Deserts**, each of which is partly located in Arizona

E is for **El Gran Cañón**, Spanish for "the Grand Canyon"

F is for **Fossils**, formed from ancient Arizona animals and plants

G is for **Golf**, played on more than 300 Arizona golf courses

H is for **Hopi Indians**, who have been in Arizona for more than 2,000 years

I is for **Indian Blanket,** a daisy-like wildflower that's red, orange & yellow

J is for **Javelina**, a pig-like animal that lives in Arizona's forests

K is for **Kiva**, a room where Native Americans hold religious ceremonies

L is for **London Bridge**, brought to Arizona from London, England

M is for **Mexico**, the country that makes up Arizona's southern border

N is for **Navajo Nation**, the largest Native American tribe in Arizona

O is for **Organ Pipe Cactus**, whose flowers only open at night

P is for **Pronghorn**, which grazes in the prairies and grasslands of Arizona

Q is for **Quartzsite**, a popular town for rock collectors to visit

R is for **Reservations**, where over 250,000 Arizona Native Americans live

S is for **Snakes**, including 11 species of rattlesnakes found in Arizona

T is for **Tucson**, where the average summer day is nearly 100 degrees

U is for the **USS Arizona**, a battleship named for the state

V is for **Verde Canyon Railroad**, where visitors take a sightseeing train ride

W is for **Window Rock**, the capital of the Navajo Nation

X is for **X Diamond Ranch**, a ranch where visitors can stay and play

Y is for **Yuma**, the sunniest town on earth

Z is for **Zeniff**, one of Arizona's many ghost towns

Grand Canyon

Over millions of years, the mighty Colorado River and its side streams cut through the rocky area of northern Arizona. The flowing water formed the Grand Canyon, 277 river miles long, up to 18 miles wide and one mile deep. Today, the Grand Canyon is one of the most beautiful sights on earth.

One of the best ways to see the Grand Canyon is on a mule ride to the bottom of the canyon.

Old Oraibi

Old Oraibi is a village of the Hopi Indians. It is more than 900 years old and is one of the oldest villages in the U.S. The Hopi lived in adobes made of clay and straw bricks. They used ladders to get "upstairs." The Hopi are peaceful people who respect the land and their way of life.

Two chiefs once settled a fight with a "push-of-war" contest, trying to push each other across a line.

Native American Tribes

```
T  J  E  S  E  M  S  H  E  E  P  P
F  L  Y  B  C  E  Y  O  Z  U  N  I
U  H  A  V  A  S  U  P  A  I  R  G
N  A  V  A  J  O  M  I  R  U  G  S
Y  P  A  K  S  C  A  K  C  H  I  N
P  A  P  A  G  O  N  O  O  U  B  M
A  C  A  I  L  R  S  R  C  A  H  O
I  H  I  B  W  N  X  N  O  L  O  J
U  E  M  A  R  I  C  O  P  A  G  A
T  M  E  B  O  D  A  L  A  P  A  V
E  T  L  M  Q  U  E  C  H  A  N  E
T  U  R  Q  U  O  I  S  E  I  D  K
```

AKCHIN	HUALAPAI	PAIUTE
APACHE	KAIBAB	PAPAGO
COCOPAH	MARICOPA	QUECHAN
HAVASUPAI	MOJAVE	YUMA
HOPI	NAVAJO	ZUNI

**Arizona has been home to many Native American tribes.
Find the tribe names above. Look for bonus words too.**

(answers on page 62)

Wyatt Earp

Many stories have been told about the Old West and its famous lawmen, explorers and cowboys. Wyatt Earp made a name for himself as a marshal and a gunman. He is best known for the "Gunfight at the O.K. Corral" in Tombstone in 1881. His brothers, his friend Doc Holliday and he faced off against a gang of outlaws.

Wyatt Earp is known for many heroic deeds, but some people wonder if his stories are true.

La Fiesta de Tumacácori

Arizona is a mixture of cultures—European, Native American, Mexican and more. For the people of the Santa Cruz Valley, that's reason to celebrate. Each December, La Fiesta de Tumacácori combines customs and traditions from all of the different heritages, with dancing, food, crafts, games and more!

Swatting a piñata is a popular Spanish game for kids. When the piñata breaks, candy pours out of it.

London Bridge

London Bridge used to be across the ocean, in London, England. How did it get to Arizona? In 1968, the founder of Lake Havasu City bought the bridge from the city of London. The famous bridge was taken apart, stone by stone. Some of the stones were shipped thousands of miles and put back together over Lake Havasu.

 Do you know the song "London Bridge Is Falling Down"? This London Bridge is in that song.

What Does Not Belong in Arizona? ⌒

Draw an X over the things you would NOT see in Arizona. Circle your favorite things about the state.

(answers on page 62)

Phoenix

Phoenix became a city in 1868, but its history goes much further back than that. The ancient Hohokam people began living in the area more than 2,000 years ago. Phoenix became the territorial capital in 1889 and has grown into the sixth-largest city in the U.S.

Phoenix is a great place for golfing. There are more than 200 golf courses, and it's sunny almost every day.

Monument Valley

Even people who have never been to Arizona recognize Monument Valley's beautiful landscape. Found on the northern border of the state, the region is famous thanks to its many appearances in movies and on TV. Its rock formations—tall stone buttes—look like huge stone castles.

Monument Valley Navajo Tribal Park lies within this region. It is like a national park of the Navajo Nation.

Arizona Crossword

Across

6. Home of "World's Oldest Rodeo"
8. State bordering Arizona
9. Native American tribe in Arizona
10. Desert plant
11. Major river flowing through Arizona
12. Arizona nickname

Down

1. Capital city of Arizona
2. Lawman Wyatt _____
3. Arizona state fish
4. Famous gymnast from Arizona
5. Large dam in Arizona
7. Largest Native American tribe in Arizona

Use the clues given above to fill in the squares of this crossword puzzle. Think hard!

(answers on page 62)

Saguaro Cactus Blossom

The Saguaro Cactus is the largest cactus in the United States. Its white blossoms are the Arizona State Flower. The cactus can live 150 to 200 years, and its flowers do not appear until the cactus is at least 35 years old. The blossoms open in the cool desert nights and close early in the morning.

The Saguaro Cactus Blossom is white with a bright yellow center, but you can color it any way you want!

Kerri Strug

Kerri Strug, from Tucson, began flipping and tumbling when she was very young. She started competing in gymnastics when she was eight. Ten years later, she helped her team win a gold medal in the 1996 Olympics—even though she was hurt. People remember her courage and spirit.

 In the 1996 Olympics, Kerri hurt her ankle. She competed anyway, helping her team win a gold medal.

Fun Food

Arizona is known for its unique Southwestern foods, which come from Native American and Mexican traditions. The recipes have been used for generations to feed families. A burrito is a popular Southwestern food. It is a soft tortilla wrapped around a mixture of ingredients like corn, beans, rice, meat and cheese.

 Build your own burrito. Color the ingredients you want in your burrito. Cross out what you don't want.

Brighty the Famous Burro

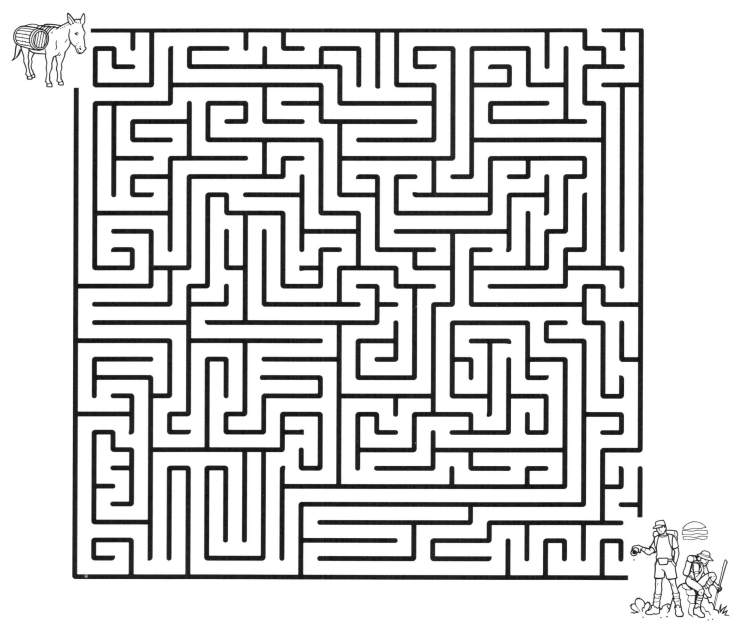

Brighty was a burro that lived and worked at the Grand Canyon in the late 1800s and early 1900s. His job was to carry water to tourists staying on the North Rim, part of the outer ring of the Grand Canyon. Books were written about this famous burro, a movie was made, and a statue was built in his honor!

The tourists are thirsty. Help Brighty find his way to them, so they can get a drink of water.

(answer on page 62)

Buffalo Soldiers

Many African Americans fought in the Indian Wars across the Southwest. The Cheyenne Indians called them "wild buffalo" because their hair looked like the hair of a buffalo, and they fought bravely like the buffalo. Soon, these great African Americans became known as Buffalo Soldiers.

Buffalo Soldiers built roads and protected wagon trains that traveled across Native American territories.

Henry Wickenburg

Henry Wickenburg came to the West looking for gold. He arrived in Arizona in 1862. As the story goes, he threw a rock at a vulture that was bothering his mule. The rock split open, and he found gold inside. He named the place Vulture Mine. The town later became known as Wickenburg.

 A sign on a bridge in Wickenburg says, "No fishing from bridge." No problem—there's no water in the river below!

Casa Grande Ruins

Archaeologists are not sure why Casa Grande was built, but they know it was very important to the ancient people of the Sonoran Desert. In 1892, it became the first archaeological reserve in the U.S. In 1918, it became a national monument. A roof was built over the ruins to protect and preserve it.

Casa Grande means "great house." Connect the dots to see what the great house might have looked like.

Kachinas

Kachinas are spirits of the Hopi Indian religion. They are thought to bring rain, healing and protection. To honor these spirits, kachina dancers wear masks during religious ceremonies, and kachina dolls are carved and given to children. This teaches them about the Hopi religion and way of life.

 Two of the kachina dolls above are exactly the same. Can you tell which ones they are? Look carefully!

(answer on page 62)

Ghost Towns

The discovery of gold in Arizona brought countless people to the region, hoping to get rich. This was called the Gold Rush, and it led to the creation of many towns. As soon as the gold was gone, people left. The towns were empty and forgotten, nicknamed "ghost towns."

Arizona has about 275 ghost towns. Some have been restored to show what the Old West was really like.

Fun with Words

Have some fun with these Arizona words. Try to use them while you're talking to someone today.

Ahehee (ah-heh-heh-eh) Navajo word for "thank you"

Chilies (chill-eez) hot peppers that are a favorite Southwestern food

Coatimundi (kot-eh-mun-dee) a mammal with a long tail and pointed white face

Cochise (ko-chees) one of the Apache's most famous chiefs

Petroglyphs (pet-row-gliffs) ancient rock drawings that tell a story

To (toe) Navajo word for "water"

Trading Post (tray-ding post) a store where people traded for food and supplies

A R I Z O N A

_____ _____ _____ _____ _____ _____

_____ _____ _____ _____ _____ _____

_____ _____ _____ _____ _____ _____

 How many different words can you make from the letters that spell "Arizona"? Write them on the blanks.

(answer on page 62)

Arizona Tree Frog

The Arizona Tree Frog is Arizona's state amphibian. Tree frogs live high up in trees, and they are very small—only up to two inches long. They have black spots on their backs and are usually green, but they can also be gold. Tree frogs eat beetles, spiders, worms and flies, while birds and snakes like to eat these frogs.

 Male tree frogs make lots of chatter in the summer, looking for females. The females do not make a sound.

Mammals of Arizona

```
G V O L E P D E E R Y M
A B C O Y O T E S V W O
B I G H O R N S H E E P
C S B O B C A T J S A R
A O J A G U A R A U S O
R N R A T P F O X O E N
J A V E L I N A N M L G
A O L R I N G T A I L H
C D S H R E W B U R R O
J A C K R A B B I T G R
B P R A I R I E D O G N
R E R A C C O O N N D A
```

BIGHORN SHEEP	FOX	PRONGHORN
BISON	JACKRABBIT	RACCOON
BOBCAT	JAGUAR	RINGTAIL
BURRO	JAVELINA	SHREW
COYOTE	PORCUPINE	VOLE
DEER	PRAIRIE DOG	WEASEL

There are 144 kinds of mammals in Arizona. Find the names of 18 mammals in the word find above.

(answers on page 62)

Spring Baseball

Professional baseball starts in April. But before that, the teams play practice games in warm-weather states. Many teams play their practice games in Arizona's Cactus League. During these spring games, coaches see the new players and decide who will be on the team when the real games begin.

 Do you like to play baseball? Do you watch it too? Who's your favorite baseball player? _____

Ringtail

The ringtail is the state mammal of Arizona. It looks a bit like a cat, but it is a relative of the raccoon. Ringtails are nocturnal, which means they are most active at night. They are omnivores, which means they eat plants and meat. They make their homes—called dens—inside trees, under rocks and in empty buildings.

Ringtails have a gray body with black and white bands of fur that make rings around their tails.

Stargazing

Have you ever looked into the sky at night to see the stars? At the Kitt Peak National Observatory, astronomers look through giant telescopes to study and learn about space. They have one of the world's largest solar telescopes. It's as tall as a large building—you can see the telescope from 50 miles away.

Tele means "far," and *skopein* means "to see." Put them together to get the word *telescope*, or "to see far."

Four Deserts

Deserts are places that get very little rain, and the U.S. has four deserts. All of them pass through Arizona. The Sonoran Desert is famous for the Saguaro Cactus. The Chihuahuan Desert is the largest in North America. The Mojave Desert has the record for being the hottest. The Great Basin Desert is a cold desert.

True or false? A cactus can survive in hot, dry weather because it doesn't need water. _____

(answer on page 62)

Old Bill Williams

William Williams, often called Old Bill Williams, was a mountain man and a trapper. He learned the ways of the Osage Indians, living with them for many years. An Arizona town and a mountain are named after Old Bill Williams, but he is better known for his tall tales and legends.

In 2006, Buff the Dog ran for mayor of Williams, Arizona. One out of every four voters voted for him!

Animals Crossword

Across

3. Colorful snake

7. Soldiers were named after them

8. State amphibian

9. "Monster" of the desert

10. Frog that lives only in Ramsey County

11. State bird

Down

1. Desert animal with pinchers and stingers

2. Wild pig-like animal

4. State mammal

5. Dog that ran for mayor of Williams, Arizona

6. Grassland and prairie animal

7. Brighty was one

Each clue above is about an animal. Use the clues to fill in the crossword squares.

(answers on page 63)

Native Arts

Native American traditions are sacred to the native peoples. Their methods for making rugs, pottery, baskets, paintings and jewelry are a few examples of their sacred traditions. The beautiful designs in their art mean something very special and can take months—even years—to create.

Look at the beautiful rugs shown above. Draw your own special pattern on the blank rug.

Biosphere 2

Biosphere 2 is a series of large, glass buildings near Tucson. It is bigger than two football fields, and scientists use it to study the way the environment affects people, plants and animals. Inside you can see a tropical rainforest, an ocean and a desert. It is a great place to learn about the earth.

Eight people once lived inside the sphere for two years without coming out. They grew their own food.

Gila Monster

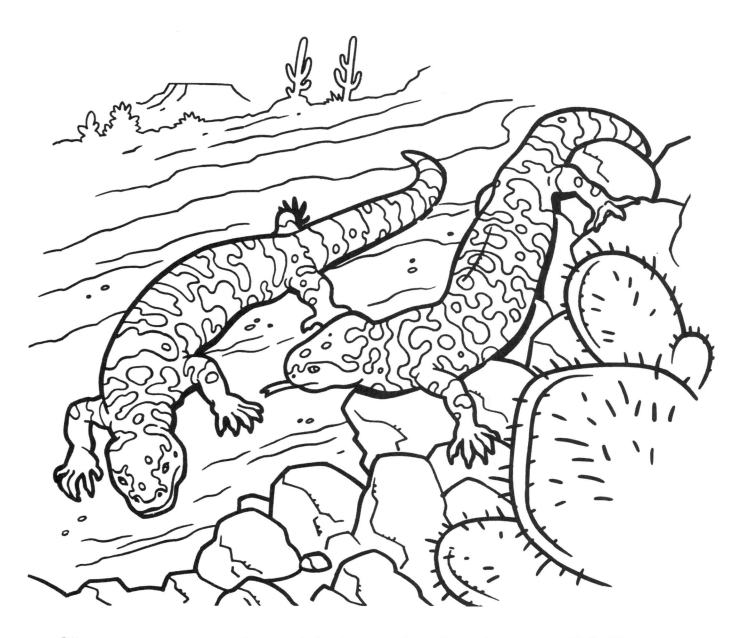

Gila monsters are reptiles and the largest lizards native to the U.S. They are black with pink, orange or yellow patterns. They can be up to two feet long and weigh as much as five pounds. Gila monsters eat eggs, young birds, insects and mice. You say Gila like, "he-luh."

Gila monsters eat large meals and store fat in their big tails, so they can go for months without eating.

Fill in the Blanks

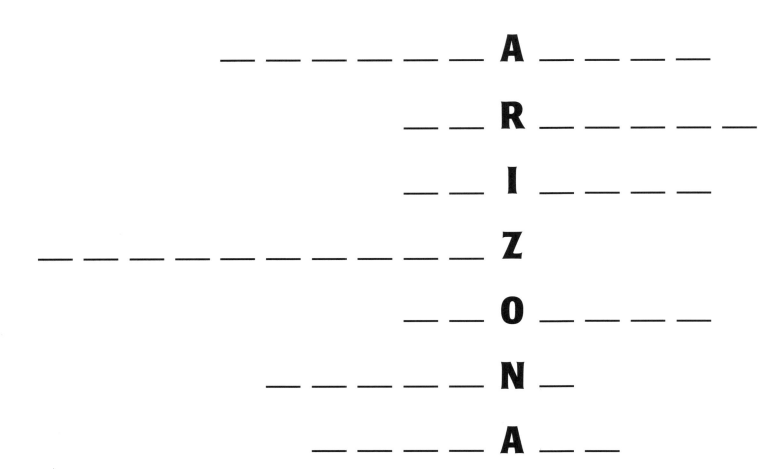

— — — — — — **A** — — — —

— — **R** — — — — —

— — **I** — — — —

— — — — — — — — — — **Z** — — — —

— — **O** — — — —

— — — — — **N** —

— — — — **A** — —

1. What is the national park that's 217 miles long and a mile deep?

2. Who was the famous leader of the Apache tribe that fought to save their lands?

3. What was the name of the burro that helped carry water to visitors?

4. Who was the famous man that helped to protect farm workers?

5. What is the capital of Arizona?

6. What are the dolls that teach children about the Hopi Indian ways?

7. On what cactus does the state flower grow?

(answers on page 63)

Geronimo

Geronimo was a leader of the Apache Nation. He fought against Mexico and the U.S., who tried to take his people's land. His real name was Goyahkla, and he was a fierce warrior. Mexican soldiers called to Saint Jerome, "Jeronimo," for help against him. That's how he got his name.

Do you have a nickname? How did you get it? If you could choose a nickname, what would it be? _____

Cinco de Mayo

Cinco de Mayo is Spanish for "the fifth of May." It is a Mexican holiday in memory of the Battle of Puebla on May 5, 1862. On that day, the Mexicans won a great battle against French invaders. The holiday is celebrated every year by many Arizonans to remember the state's Mexican heritage.

 Holidays are an important way to remember the past. What's your favorite holiday? _____

Pima Air and Space Museum

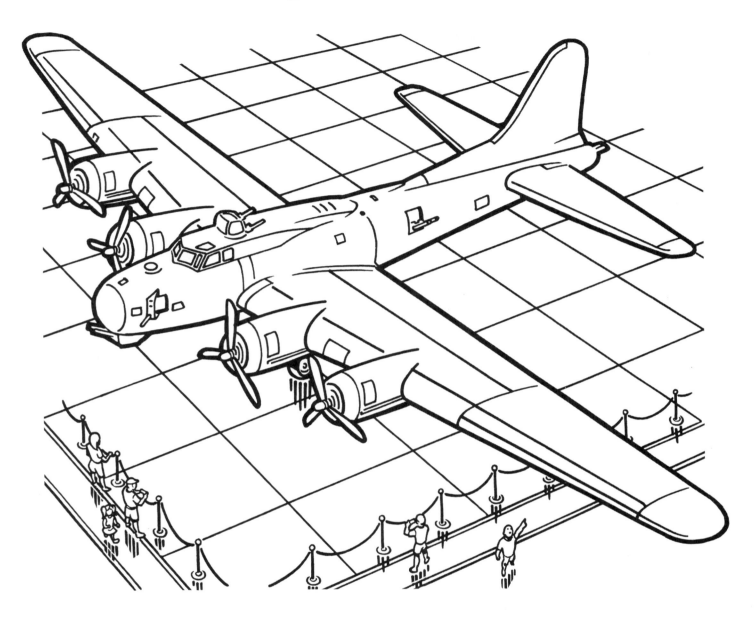

Pima Air and Space Museum, in Tucson, is one of the largest air and space museums in the world. It has more than 300 airplanes and spacecraft to see. Many of the aircraft were very important to the history of our country. In fact, one of them is former President John F. Kennedy's airplane, *Air Force One*.

 The B-17, also called "The Flying Fortress," is a U.S. bomber that flew during World War II.

Cactus of Arizona

```
L  D  C  O  Y  O  T  E  H  M  U  V
B  C  H  J  U  M  P  I  N  G  S  O
N  P  R  I  C  K  L  Y  P  E  A  R
O  I  I  P  C  J  O  B  I  B  G  G
I  N  S  A  A  B  C  E  N  P  U  A
P  E  T  G  W  A  O  E  C  A  A  N
R  A  M  A  S  R  T  H  U  N  R  P
O  P  A  V  N  R  I  I  S  C  O  I
C  P  S  E  A  E  L  V  H  A  C  P
S  L  R  F  K  L  L  E  I  K  K  E
H  E  D  G  E  H  O  G  O  E  S  G
L  I  Z  A  R  D  P  E  N  C  I  L
```

AGAVE	JUMPING	PINCUSHION
BARREL	OCOTILLO	PINEAPPLE
BEEHIVE	ORGAN PIPE	PRICKLY PEAR
CHRISTMAS	PANCAKE	SAGUARO
HEDGEHOG	PENCIL	YUCCA

**Arizona is well known for its many varieties of cactus.
Find the names of 15 common cacti in this word find.**

(answers on page 63)

Meteor Crater

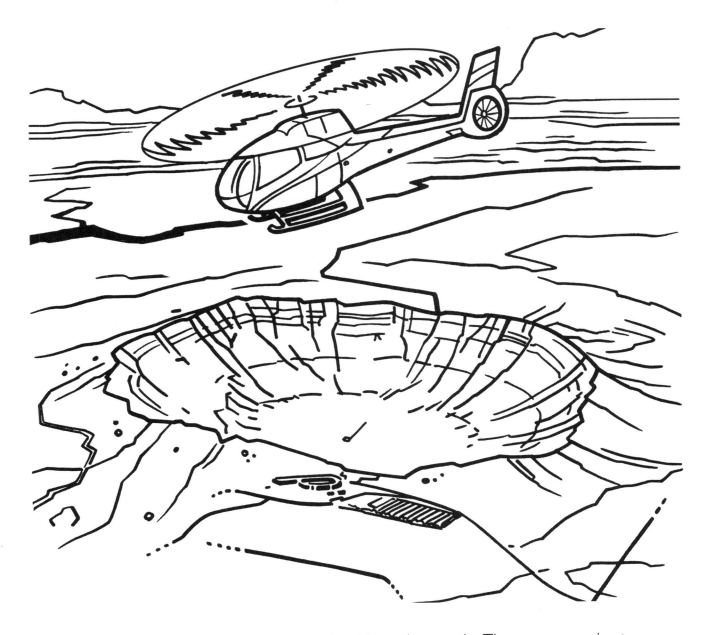

Thousands of years ago, a meteor crashed into the earth. There was a giant explosion of rock and dirt, making a hole in the ground about 550 feet deep and one mile across. The bottom of the crater is big enough to hold 20 football fields! We call this large, bowl-shaped hole Meteor Crater, and it's a great place to visit.

At Meteor Crater's visitor center, you can watch a movie about how the crater was formed.

Four Corners Monument

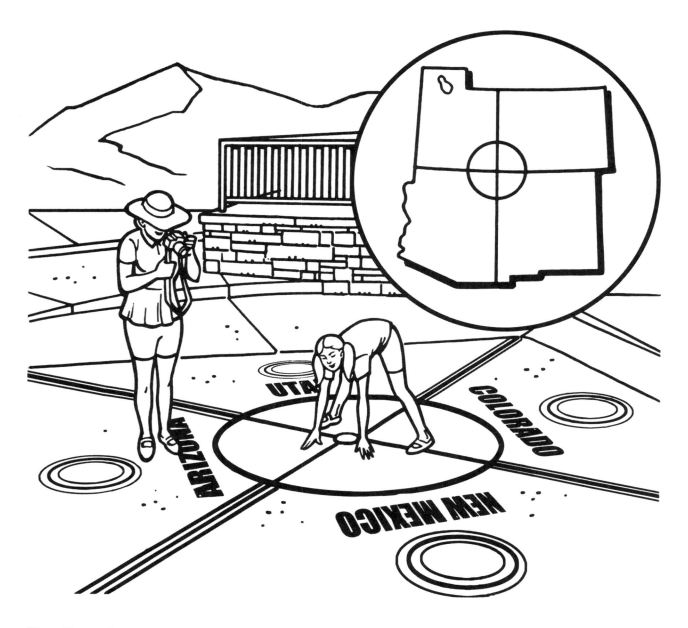

The Four Corners Monument is the only place in the United States where four states meet at one point. The corners of Arizona, Colorado, New Mexico and Utah all touch there. The monument lies within the land of the Navajo Nation, which takes care of this unique location.

 In the center of the monument, you can get your picture taken touching all four states at one time!

Park Rules

Camping in Arizona's state and national parks can be a great way to spend your vacation. The parks were made for us to enjoy, with opportunities for swimming, hiking, marshmallow roasting and sleeping under the stars. Remember to respect other campers, the park and the animals.

Rules help to keep everyone safe. Circle the things above that are not safe or are against the rules.

(answers on page 62)

Hoover Dam

Hoover Dam is on the Colorado River, on the border of Arizona and Nevada. The dam is made out of concrete and is 660 feet thick at the bottom. It holds back the water of Lake Mead. Water rushes past Hoover Dam's 17 generators, making electricity for more than 25 million people in Arizona, Nevada and California.

Lake Mead holds trillions of gallons of water. It took two years to fill the lake after the dam was built.

Copper Mining

Copper in Arizona was first used by Native Americans. Early Spanish explorers also discovered this valuable metal. Later, after the railroads were built, copper helped Arizona grow into the state it is today. Now Arizona produces more copper than all of the other states combined. The industry gives jobs to many workers.

You may not see copper, but you use it every day in computers, refrigerators, phones, cars and more!

Archaeology

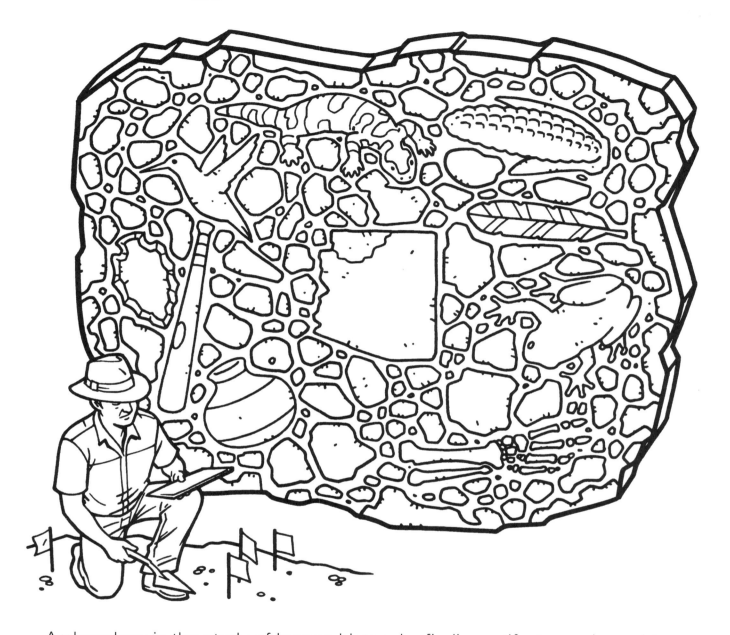

Archaeology is the study of human history by finding artifacts, such as old bones, tools, dishes and jewelry. We know a lot about Arizona's history thanks to discoveries by archaeologists digging around ancient ruins. Artifacts are studied and kept so we can better understand Arizona's past.

What objects can you find hidden in the picture above about Arizona and its people? Color them.

(answers on page 63)

Route 66

When early settlers started moving west, trails used by explorers became roads for wagon trains. Many of the roads later turned into highways and interstates. Route 66 is a famous road that passes through eight states. It is featured in a number of songs and movies, such as Disney's *Cars*.

Circle the Grand Canyon State. What other states does Route 66 pass through? _____

Navajo Bridge

The Navajo Bridge crosses the Colorado River at the east end of the Grand Canyon. The original bridge was completed in 1929, and a new bridge was built beside it in 1995. The Navajo Bridge is one of only two ways within 600 miles to drive across the canyon and the river.

 For a thrill, professional bungee jumpers sometimes jump off the bridge while tied to a bungee cord.

Canyon de Chelly National Monument

Canyon de Chelly (pronounced "canyon da-shay") National Monument is made up of beautiful canyons, red rock cliffs and ruins of ancient peoples. They built their homes into the cliff walls, using timber and adobe bricks. Today, Canyon de Chelly is one of the best archaeological sites in the U.S.

What did these ancient dwellings look like? Connect the dots to find out!

Cesar Chavez

Mexican-Americans work in farmers' fields to harvest fruits and vegetables. They are called migrant workers. Cesar Chavez was a migrant worker from Arizona. He saw that the workers weren't always treated fairly. He worked hard after World War II to get better working conditions and better pay for migrant workers.

Cesar had a motto, or special saying. It was "Si, se puede." That's Spanish for, "Yes, it is possible."

Petrified Forest National Park

Millions of years ago, the area now called the Petrified Forest National Park
was swamp land. When trees in the swamp fell, mud and sand covered them.
Minerals in the water and mud soaked into the wood. When the wood dried,
the minerals turned to stone. So petrified wood is "wood turned to stone."

 **In the picture, there is a fossil of a small, two-footed
dinosaur. Can you find it?**

Cattle Ranch

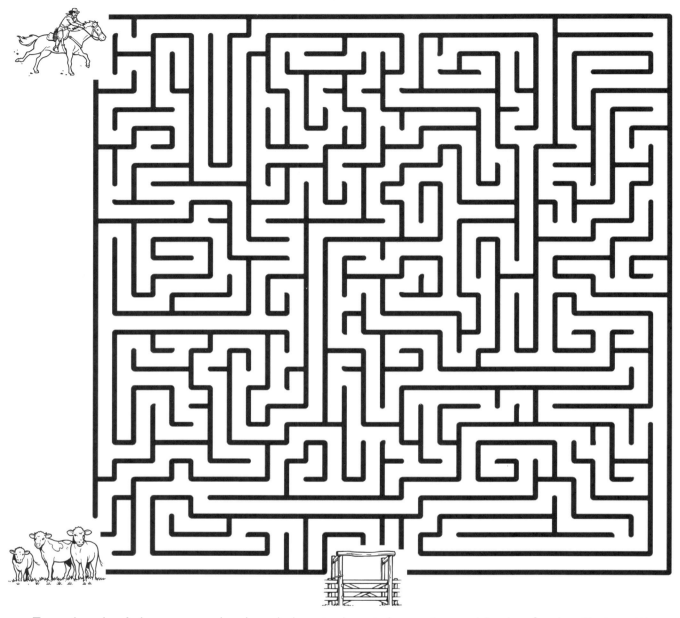

Farming in Arizona can be hard due to heat, insects and lack of rain. But cattle ranches are successful because of Arizona's excellent grazing land. Today, guest ranches welcome visitors to experience ranch life. Cowboys are still seen driving cattle, fixing fences and riding the range like in the Old West.

Help the cowboy get through the maze, first to the cattle and then to the ranch.

(answer on page 63)

Flagstaff

Flagstaff is called Arizona's winter playground. Even though it is hot in the summer, winter can bring more than 100 inches of snow to the San Francisco Peaks near Flagstaff. People come from all over the world to ski, and those who live in the desert find Flagstaff a very "cool" place to be.

 In 1973, Flagstaff got 210 inches of snow. That would make a lot of snowballs!

Arizona Bingo

If you see one of the people, places, animals or objects on the bingo card, mark it with an X. Be sure to mark the free space in the middle. If you get five Xs in a row, you win! Remember to yell "Bingo!"

B	I	N	G	O
CACTUS	BURRO	PETRIFIED WOOD	HOOVER DAM	KACHINA DOLL
ROUTE 66 SIGN	NAVAJO BRIDGE	NATIVE POTTERY	HOT AIR BALLOON	SOMBRERO
RATTLESNAKE	HUMMINGBIRD	FREE	HORSE	TREE FROG
BASEBALL PLAYER	PRAIRIE DOG	BIGHORN SHEEP	FOUR CORNERS	EAGLE
AIRPLANE	FOSSIL	STATE FLAG	TELESCOPE	COWBOY

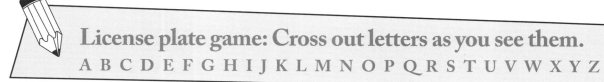

License plate game: Cross out letters as you see them.

A B C D E F G H I J K L M N O P Q R S T U V W X Y Z

Code Talkers

During World War II in the 1940s, U.S. soldiers had trouble getting secret messages to each other. Enemy troops would steal the messages and know what was going to happen next. The U.S. began to use Navajo "code talkers" to send messages using their ancient Navajo language. It worked!

Chay-da-gahi is the Navajo word for tortoise. It meant "tank." *Besh-lo* meant "iron fish," or "submarine."

Ramsey Canyon

Ramsey Canyon is in the Huachuca (wa-chew-ka) Mountains in southeastern Arizona. It is a beautiful place to visit, hike and explore. There are many different kinds of plants and animals in the canyon. The cool canyon walls are also famous for at least 15 different kinds of hummingbirds.

 The Ramsey Canyon Leopard Frog is only found in the area of Ramsey Canyon.

Quiz Your Parents

1. What states border Arizona?

2. What is Arizona's state nickname?

3. What is the capital of Arizona?

4. What is the state gemstone of Arizona?

5. What is the highest point in Arizona?

6. What were the Navajo men who helped during World War II called?

7. What is the name of the famous dam on the border of Arizona and Nevada?

8. How did the trees in the Petrified Forest turn to stone?

9. What four states can you touch all at the same time?

10. What mineral is mined more in Arizona than in any other state?

11. What holiday is celebrated on May 5th in Arizona?

12. What are the names of the four deserts that pass through Arizona?

13. What is the state mammal, sometimes mistaken for a raccoon?

14. How many pennies would equal the copper on the State Capitol's roof?

15. What famous children's song mentions a bridge in Arizona?

16. Who was Wyatt Earp's best friend?

17. What animal ran for Mayor of Williams, Arizona?

18. What sport do "snowbirds" come to watch in the spring?

19. Who is the famous Arizona gymnast that helped her team win a gold medal?

20. What are the four major professional sports teams in Arizona?

(answers on page 63)

Arizona Coral Snake

Arizona Coral Snakes are colorful reptiles found in Arizona. They can be 13 to 21 inches long and are known for their red, black and yellow rings. They are venomous snakes, and they like to eat other snakes and lizards. They come out after the sun goes down and usually stay active during the night.

Color the areas above using the following code:
1 = red, 2 = black, 3 = yellow

Name the Animals

1. _____

2. _____

3. _____

4. _____

5. _____

6. _____

7. _____

8. _____

Name the animals you might see in Arizona.

(answers on page 63)

Answers

Page 3—Arizona Map

1. Colorado River
2. Five
3. California, New Mexico, Colorado, Nevada, Utah

Page 9—Native American Tribes

T	J	E	S	E	M	S	H	E	E	P	P
F	L	Y	B	C	E	Y	O	Z	U	N	I
U	H	A	V	A	S	U	P	A	I	R	G
N	A	V	A	J	O	M	I	R	U	G	S
Y	P	A	K	S	C	A	K	C	H	I	N
P	A	P	A	G	O	N	O	O	U	B	M
A	C	A	I	L	R	S	R	C	A	H	O
I	H	I	B	W	N	X	N	O	L	O	J
U	E	M	A	R	I	C	O	P	A	G	A
T	M	E	B	O	D	A	L	A	P	A	V
E	T	L	M	Q	U	E	C	H	A	N	E
T	U	R	Q	U	O	I	S	E	I	D	K

Bonus words:
Hogan, Corn, Turquoise, Sheep
Super bonus = Adobe (backwards)

Page 13—What Does Not Belong in Arizona?

Pyramids, whale, cruise ship, volcano

Page 16—Arizona Crossword

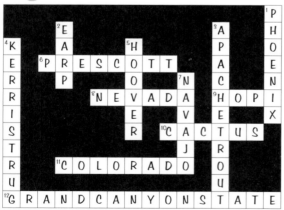

Page 45—Park Rules

axe in tree, dog off leash, garbage by tent, fire not watched, fire outside fire pit, swimming kids not watched, loud music, spilled drink not cleaned up

Page 20—Brighty the Famous Burro

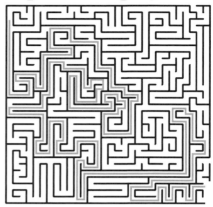

Page 24—Kachinas

Page 26—Fun with Words

A, air, an, I, in, ion, iron, no, noir, nor, oar, on, or, oz, rain, ran

Page 28—Mammals of Arizona

G	V	O	L	E	P	D	E	E	R	Y	M
A	B	C	O	Y	O	T	E	S	V	W	O
B	I	G	H	O	R	N	S	H	E	E	P
C	S	B	O	B	C	A	T	J	S	A	R
A	O	J	A	G	U	A	R	A	U	S	O
R	N	R	A	T	P	F	O	X	O	E	N
J	A	V	E	L	I	N	A	N	M	L	G
A	O	L	R	I	N	G	T	A	I	L	H
C	D	S	H	R	E	W	B	U	R	R	O
J	A	C	K	R	A	B	B	I	T	G	R
B	P	R	A	I	R	I	E	D	O	G	N
R	E	R	A	C	C	O	O	N	N	D	A

Bonus words:
Ape, Rat
Super Bonus = Mouse (backwards)

Page 32—Four Deserts

False—a cactus needs water; it stores water in its stem

Answers

Page 34–Animals Crossword

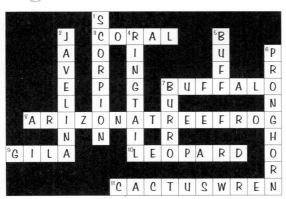

Page 38–Fill in the Blanks

1. Grand Canyon
2. Geronimo
3. Brighty
4. Cesar Chavez
5. Phoenix
6. Kachina
7. Saguaro

Page 42–Cactus of Arizona

Bonus words:
Rocks, Snake, Coyote, Lizard
Super Bonus = Scorpion (backwards)

Page 48–Archaeology

Arizona, baseball bat, clay pot, corn on the cob, feather, frog, Gila monster, hummingbird, spearhead, bones

Page 49–Route 66

California   Oklahoma   New Mexico
Kansas   Missouri
Texas   Illinois

Page 54–Cattle Ranch

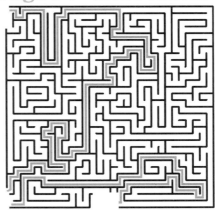

Page 59–Quiz Your Parents

1. California, Nevada, Utah, Colorado, New Mexico
2. The Grand Canyon State
3. Phoenix
4. Turquoise
5. Humphrey's Peak, 12,633 feet
6. Code Talkers
7. Hoover Dam
8. Minerals inside the wood crystallized
9. Utah, Colorado, New Mexico, Arizona
10. Copper
11. Cinco de Mayo
12. Sonoran, Great Basin, Mojave, Chihuahuan
13. Ringtail
14. 4,800,000 (4 million, 800 thousand)
15. London Bridge Is Falling Down
16. Doc Holliday
17. Buff the Dog
18. Baseball
19. Kerri Strug
20. Arizona Diamondbacks, Phoenix Coyotes, Arizona Cardinals, Phoenix Suns

Page 61–Name the Animals

1. Coyote
2. Burro
3. Cougar
4. Bison
5. Bighorn Sheep
6. Porcupine
7. Prairie Dog
8. Bear

About the Author

Paula Ellis grew up in a small town in central Michigan. Her love of the outdoors and travel began at a young age. She is the mother of two children, daughter Heather and son Todd David. Through travel and everyday experiences, she taught them to appreciate, respect and enjoy all of creation.

Paula enjoys being a grandma, exploring the wilderness, traveling and watching her four grandchildren grow and learn about the world in which they live.

She believes children are eager to learn about their environment, whether they're playing in the backyard, traveling across the country or catching bugs on a camping trip. To that end, she strives to encourage children of all ages to see and explore all of the fascinating things around them.

Every now and then you will find her standing in the lake at sunset, fishing.

About the Illustrator

Picking up a pencil and drawing on a sheet of paper is one of Shane's first memories, and he has never stopped since! It was no surprise when at a very young age he decided that artwork would be more than his hobby; it would be his lifelong career.

Shane has been fortunate enough to work on many exciting projects in many different fields: from t-shirt designs to comic books and from science fiction paintings to movie storyboards. He has always had a soft spot for making artwork that children can enjoy.

Shane found his home in Portland, OR. He has a wonderful daughter Hannah who has the potential to be a great artist if she works hard. The same can be said for you, no matter what it is you want to do.